Sweet and Sour Candy

Candy

Print information available on the last page

Rev. date: 06/13/2019

To order additional copies of this book, contact:
Xlibris
1-888-795-4274
www.Xlibris.com
Orders@Xlibris.com

Contents

I Am She!

Once I wuz but not who I really wuz, just becuz I didn't want to make a fuzz to my family and cuz about who I really wuz, just want to be luved my me who duz and anyone else who duz!

Just A Name

A name is just a name,

It is used, sometimes abused,

Two of same name makes me confused!

Why me to blame?!?

Even a famed name is still the same,

Faces and dates have I no shame!

Easy to the muse

But a name is just a name just the same!

Von Dem Ist Die Liebe?

Warum würden Sie noch ein neues Leben begehren?

Was könnte das Leben uns in dieser Welt lehren?

Nach der Liebe von Gott und unseren Eltern sollen wir immer trachten!

Solche eine Antwort ist leicht zu merken und auch zu beobachten.

Dann die Liebe wird am jeden Menschen in erfüllung vermehren!

'würden, könnte and erfüllung are correct now with the dots over the u, o and the u'

'die Liebe wird is changed from wird die Liebe'

'title added'

Words Of Me

Words love I
Words excite my oh my
Words eat I
Kids cereal prefer I,
such a kid am I
Full of sugar, high am I,
but alphabet cereal bought I
Now want I only to reflect and sigh!

The life of a plaid jacket on a hanger

A coat of not so many colours,

Standing out like a sore thumb from all the others.

Worn by a manly man from northern Canada, who chopped wood for survival

whilst accompanied by his lady Amanda.

'Till a concubine became his desire,

and Amanda's heart sad with raging fire 🔥!

Stole his plaid jacket and surrendered it to a 2nd hand store, only to have it placed

on a hanger to even the score! 🕴

A Dixie chick from scratch

This lil' chick didn't know it yet but it would soon become quite the catch!

Mrs. Hen is sitting on her young, feeling excited, can't wait for her chick to hatch.

Whilst Mr. Rooster 🐔 perched on a fence, makes the morning call, as though no one could tell time at all!

Suddenly, the lil' chick breaks from its shell 🐚 without a hitch or a scratch and joins the fellow chicks 🐥🐥🐥 who all resemble each other like a perfect match.

Milling about under a heat lamp light, they chirp and squeal, looking so cool 😎!

Safe in their chicken coop Palace that looks more like a Kindergarten school.

It came to pass that in a little while that Dixie chick 🐤 became a full grown chicken 🐓 and couldn't wait to cross the road!

Why did the chicken cross the road?

To avoid KFC of course! ♀♀

L'Amour Est Là!

C'est là où l'amour existe!
Ce n'est pas là la loi le prescrit.
C'est là où mon coeur n'est pas fini,
dans la tête où le désir suffit
et de la bouche où les mots expliquent!
C'est là où l'amour
commence ici!

The love, the beauty and the fake!

This church is made brick and mortar that one can call God's home But within these walls, lies some regulations that fill the congregation with only hearts of stone!
All walks of life are beautiful and equal in God's eyes And no one is better than anybody else even in children's eyes!
Where the LGBT community should be accepted and celebrated, but only the 4th part of this group is ever tolerated!
Too bad, so sad, I wish that this were just a silly fad, Replied little spurned happy Mac to his dad.

Mickey Ist Bereit!

Im Frühling ist der Vogel (Mickey) bereit zu fliegen!

Mit bunten Federn und glühenden Augen fühlt der sich völlig stark zu siegen.

Vor einem Jahr hat der Traum angefangen daß der Vogel endlich keine Angst

haben würdet, zu verlassen um Essen zu fangen!

Jetzt ist er fertig und das Wetter ist barmherzig,

Prima! Der Vogel (Mickey) hat absolut geflogen leider fand er sich zu schnell auf

dem Boden!

♀😎

17

I Beseech Thee!

Wherefore hast thou done this thing unto me?

Shew thy true self and be thou of a good cheer!

I shalt make mine abode with thee.

Lo, I fashion a resting place betwixt thee and me.

Doth not my company dissipate any fear?

Whence I leave, I wit not!

Peradventure 'till the dawn of a new day bringeth forth happy thoughts that they might enter the head therein.

The New Look

Sue: How do you like your new look?

Jane: Could I have the mirror?

Sue: Sure sweetie!

Jane: OMG!

My hair looks like Buckwheat's hair in the 1930s if he had the mange?!?
My lips look like protruding lips of Howard The Duck from 1987?!?
And my eyes bulge out like the villain from 1990s Total Recall near the end when he was gasping for air!

Sue: Soooo, you're not pleased?!?

Jane: r u kidding? I love it!

Sue: Oooookaaaaay!

La Lune occupée

Je ne peux pas attendre la voir!

Le temps s'arrive et je suis entièrement prêt ce soir.

La Terre est toute passée et la Lune sera finalement occupée Je vais voler à la lune sans ailes comme Le Petit Prince lequel j'ai lu dans l'école.

Reste là toute seule pas de bruits ni des personnes un peu et mange du fromage sur la lune bleu!

Si on a soif? On pourrait boire du lait de La Voie Lactée!

Ce qu'est une merveilleuse vie vous croyez?!?

Legs Have It

I got legs just like the video from ZZ Top!

Slender, smooth and freshly waxed from my toes to the top!

Sensuous, irresistible and slightly burnished like a porcelain dolly, a vision of a long

cool woman from the popular song of The Hollies!

I dance, prance and move about with my legs 'cause they're mine to own!

One could say that I'm feeling satisfaction as the classic song by The Rollin' Stones!

I Take A Break!

I don't want to be fake, for goodness sake!

Being around phony people is all I can take!

Find me by the quiet and calm lake,

for goodness sake!

Or on the beach getting my skin ready to bake, Don't even bother me for a stupid date, I promptly told Jake!

Need I not a mate but me time is what I need to make!

Until I awake, I say good night to all for pete's sake! Lol

Nida und Emma

Two little German girls skipping and hopping as they make return home from school, Hand and hand with matching plaid skirts and blond hair they converse in their mother tongue that sounds so cool!

The smell of freshly baked pie is wafting through the air of their Oma's kitchen and at the dinner table, Opa is admiring the tasty Schnitzel, Wurst and the succulent white and dark meat of a juicy chicken.

Nida and Emma came home in time with Bread and Croissants which they bought from the German store.

Now the Schmitz family is ready to feast after they bow their heads in thanks for the food, the drinks and being together forever more!

Red Army

No swagger nor a hint of hesitation, these little critters move with stealth to their certain destination!

Brave as a Canadian soldier on foot, so fierce and very determined to feast on some tasty treats!

Smaller than a size of a dime, the red marching ants have a knack for being unwelcome guests all the time!

Until these fiends met their fate one day after having been stomped on by a stranger along the way!

Free To Roam

My hometown is where I want to roam, no confusion, no isolation and no charges to my IPhone cause I need not to roam!

Where cows gather in the pasture and in the fields that buffalo would even roam!

Small round shaped houses that look more like miniature domes.

A place where I can call home with peace and happiness that fills me 'cause I am free to roam!

I Await Upon Thee

Whence comest thou unto my place?

I am of a surety that mine eyes shall put gladness in thine heart.

Upon the hearth I will make ready cakes for thee!

Lo, the day is half spent and the sun waxeth hot!

Hasten thyself to come unto me.

Art thou not beaten down and stained with travel?

I tarry for thee 'till the hour doth come and we can be merry whilst the day still bringeth forth light!

A Friend For You

Burden yourself not with that situation anymore and tell yourself that it's time to let it go!
When you reached rock bottom 'cause you are feeling at an all time low, let me mend your broken heart and fix your torn coat with sew.
I am a friend indeed whom you can trust and certainly not a foe!
Come here and I will help you to make it so that you can follow me like a comforted friend in toe!

Door ajar

Like a pendulum that swings back and forth with a quiet rhythm of its own, the hinges on the door of my heart open up to receive friends herein and close to the unwanted and the unknown! As the door of a car that only opens so far and remains totally ajar, my happy red heart will only allow so much pain by far and won't be left unguarded to face a possible permanent scar!

Lest I appear to be a bit crass or cold, there are no special keys to my heart for you to take hold so don't bother to even moan or grope then 'cause the back door to my welcoming heart is always open!

Poor Tom did it again

Plucks the white lace ankle socks off the close line, Encasing his pedicured feet with them to feel so fine!

Nite after nite, neighbors stockings become missing, in his room many beige pantyhose are strewn everywhere!

Daring to gird his loins up with a black and silky pair, Tom even musters up the courage to go drag while driving his car!

But continuously is petrified by what society might think by going this far!

The neighbors all understand about his borrowing habits stockings fetishes, If only poor Tom knew that he would be accepted and could be proud of his female style that he relishes!

A Change Of Plans

Shuffling along the tiled kitchen floor in her fluffy slippers, she reaches for the door!
Hoping to find her secret guest whom she's been thinking about and impatiently waiting for!

But instead, it's the man with the shiny band in his hand whom she promised to be with in front of the alter stand that was witnessed by all the family and friends in the Talbot land!

Feeling slightly taken aback, she reaches for the sugar container on the kitchen rack! Coffee is what the poor lady lacks to calm her unsettling nerves before she has a major panic attack!

But as the lid of the sugar container is lifted away, she discovers no sugar cubes but rather a little note from her husband that had this to say,… ' I met your male friend on the way and we hit it off 'cause we both feel the same way, bisexual and that's the way it's going to stay!'

Against ourselves

My back is against the wall,

asking for a bank loan as I feel about two feet tall!

The loan officer, she says that she's been in my shoes but simply tells me that no can do!

Transgendering is not a choice, I found myself and I'll tell anyone with my loud voice!

It is shocking to be labelled by someone in a respected profession whose ancestors have felt the pain of oppression!

Acceptance from family and friends is such a big deal 'cause they know exactly how I feel!

But sometimes even siblings worry more about self image and thus dividing the family like a game of scrimmage!

Grade School Blues

So many years later, I find myself returning to the place that as a youth, I couldn't wait to say, see ya later alligator!

Flood of memories which now are not so bad, only reminded me of how scared, timid and inferior I felt as a kid, kind of sad!

Students, parents of students and teachers used to get involved with events while I watched with a sheepish smile and remained silent in my invisible tent!

No backbone, an abundance of twisted nerves and too petrified to voice an opinion in class and barely existing as l tagged along with my fellow classmates to attend a Catholic Church mass!

But as little boys and girls, we were all very young, innocent and somewhat apprehensive!

It is pleasing to know, nowadays that I was not the only one who faced fear and uncertainty, even now when I see my ol' jail school and become a little pensive!

Laugh At Own Will

Running to the Chester drawer of my mother's youthful years, I stealthily slipped into beige stockings and poodle skirts from the 50s without a tremble or fear! Ofttimes, urges come and go, dressing up in full regalia of my mom's 80s outfits, provide temporary satisfaction 'till the feeling deflates and I snap out of it! Now, living on my own, I have free reign to explore my sexuality and to push the envelope even further by applying makeup and bracing the real me which is by far a lovelier reality!

Used To The Renewed

Whatever is the big deal to admit owning a second hand or used item, whether it be a trinket or an article of clothing?

I shame myself not nor do I pretend to have spent a fortune and bought only new at a fancy store for either of them!

Just as well with my friends whom I adore from my childhood to my adult years, there is no limit on any friendship of mine!

Old memories and new ones are built and cherished 'cause all my friends ol' and new I hold so dear!

Nobody has diplomatic immunity under the law of the land of the Lord's paradise in the sky!

We are all like used or second hand children in God's eyes without whom we could not be made renewed through Jesus, our Saviour. Our life would be just one big lie or like a pie in the sky!

Stoic Not On Purpose

Silence can be bliss depending on the mood for a human or even an animal.

Feelings are sometimes open to be shown on purpose or maybe not, one cannot always recall!

It's difficult to praise family members to others even to strangers when the same isn't done in return!

That stings or hurts as well as well in silence! It's enough to make your stomach churn! Yearning for acceptance but only to be rejected or spurned and that causes the nerves to burn!

I'm not a stoic nor do I desire any glory, inner suffering destroys as much as the exterior can when physical harm is proposed, I suppose?!?

I harm my family not!

I am not them nor are they me but we are we under the one word, Love!

Introvert am I oftentimes only because I find peace with my inner self and content like a true lonesome dove!

'Cause Jack Can!

Wow! Jackie's a man, I also heard that he's thee Man!

That's what I told Dan, who is a big fan of the Jack the Man!

Like Bo Jackson, Jack can play many sports as l watch him from the stands!

An immature kid, he is not but he likes his Apple Jacks cereal a lot!

Almost a rock star is Jack the Man, he beats on the garbage cans like Pete Best, a British drummer! Man oh Man!

Now Jack takes some beans from his hands and tosses them wherever he can, only to discover a tree in his play land!

So he decides to climb it simply 'cause Jack can!

Red Alert/ Scam Alert

An older gentleman waltzes in the place with a worried look on his face!

Approaches the counter of the Stationary Pad, he wants to send money A.S.A.P. to prevent his agent from becoming stock raving mad!

To Africa with urgency as though it be some kind of an emergency!

The store owner refuses the command in order to save the poor gentleman's cash at hand.

No gratification nor any appreciation, not even a look of relief!

He just glances at the store owner forlornly and leaves the Stationary in much disbelief.

Change Of Host

From less macho to more sensitive, this is the start of my new body!

Old parts become new again under a new name of my now feminine body.

Incisions made, twin spheres extracted and excess skin is removed.

An extra circumcision, tiny holes are bored and the manly hood is inverted and moved!

Thus, the convex package is converted into a concave organ!

Appearance, pleasure and function are reached again!

Healing, lubricating and dilating become a displeasing necessity for a short while.

The satisfaction of feeling 100 percent female is priceless and to have friends who support me, puts upon my face a sweet smile!

Lady Jane My Sister

Little Jane walks down the hall of St. Jude private school and feels her face blush as the other girls just smirk and stare!

She is bedecked in a purple plaid skirt with white laced stockings and a pink bow in her hair.

As I watch Jane go by, I can't help but to feel her isolation and sympathy for her! It matters to me that she knows how much I value friendship and I do care for her!

We became the best of friends, Jane and I, from private school catholic girls to two young beautiful ladies!

She is like an adopted sister that I never had and I'd protect her from any bullies because I adore Jane, my lady!

Spontaneous Introduction

The Mall is a thrilling place to be,

People of all walks of life are beautiful from what I can see.

The food court is inviting with many selections of foreign flavours and on a couple of occasions have I done myself and complete strangers a big favour!

I've sat with them at the eating tables, striking up a conversation or two and getting to know new faces just 'cause I'm willing and able!

It felt wonderful making new friends and I've witnessed grace in their eyes to no end!

Taking the time for someone rather than yourself is a compassionate and an altruistic act.

Simple deeds when done sincerely can bring peace of mind and a joy to others and that's a fact!

Don't Forget About It!

Forget I thee not, unless my friendship be fake which it is not!

Happy to have met you.

Let our friendship pursue and bloom like the raging waters of a monsoon .

Love you like a sister who has not been forgotten and time has no place to make it forgotten.

Friendship hold I so dear and the end is not even close to being a near!

Gimme some!

My drawers are lacking bas culottes

And those are the articles of clothing need I lots!

That's French for pantyhose!

A not so common word I suppose!

Control- Top pair desire I not

But support I want and from my mediate family receive I not!

So, gimme some

beige style stockings to fit!

Lest I feel incomplete and that's not easy to admit?!?

Slick Cowboy

The ideal cowboy usually exists in my day dream!

It commences as a sensuous fantasy when I apply makeup and a little facial cream.

Imagining his release, doused all over my face as we sit to an intimate dinner at his place.

His manscaped physique showing slightly through the half buttoned down flannel shirt that could make any woman weak in the knees!

He caresses my hair and nibbles on one of my ears 'till I am well pleased!

With the scent of men's after shave, he uses his rope to wrangle me into submission!

Then removes the cowboy hat and loosens his jeans to reveal the partial briefs which makes a dreamy vision!

Finally we ride off into the sunset on his huge stallion with my arms wrapped around my muscular and macho Italian!

Whose Gun?

What a turn off, futile to say the least!

Words and ideas am I, no thrill in harming a defenceless beast!

All makes and sizes of killing machines with one result, a senseless death left at the scene!

Hunting for survival is human nature and a right but murdering for a mere pleasure is not a pretty sight!

Guns are just tools, they don't kill, humans are the only race that destroy each other! How does that make you feel?

A fun and healthy sport gun shoot practicing can be and learning to handle a lethal weapon for self defence are acceptable to me.

A gun or a bow and arrow I will more than likely never own but a pen and paper in hand is something that I will probably be best known!

When Kitties Attack!

From a tabby or fluffy to even a Siamese, cats are so beautiful and adorable!

But if one encroaches their territory or aggravates them to the fullest, the outcome can be rather horrible!

An adult cat is more wise but takes much more naps than a baby kitten but both these animals can be on the attack if they are frightened or smitten.

Never a time are these felines considered as a watch cat even if some are colossal or just plain fat!

Fangs and claws can be a bit intimidating but they are quite helpful for meal time or when the next prey is awaiting!

Stray cats or family pets, these wonderful creatures may seem too innocent and kind but if one steps on their tail, a deafening screech or a vicious attack is what one might just find!

My True Self

I love writing silly poems and weird antedotes!
Words borrow I not,
all my from own thoughts,
Lest one might guess,
Me and myself lives to express!
Need I not to boast,
methinks worthy of a toast, ☺ happy my life destitute of no fame,
just realizing my true self and Candy's the name! 🤾🎉

Standing My Ground!

Check me out!

Don't chuck me in!

I finally came out,

no more ducking in!

I'm all decked out,

wearing what's totally the new in!

Best to spread out,

'cause this chicky knows where she's been.

Female power is on full tilt and all out!

No backing down or giving in.

I'm here to stay and there's no doubt,

I'm feeling much better and stronger within!

So Fetish Have I!

Girding up my loins with reinforced panty and toe, fulfilling my desire from head to toe!
Encasing my waxed legs in beige pantyhose, makes them complete!
Neither tights nor thigh highs could ever compete!
Lacey and white cuffed sockets are a definite turn on with a short mini skirt as a substitute to wearing nylons!

Shoo Away!

I'm a sure shoo in with respect to shoes!

Some are aware that I put my foot in my mouth when I talk about my shoes.

Ladies flats and high heels are my fav!

To own my own shoe store, I'd almost surrender all I have!

A down payment just to get my foot in the door that would be a wonderful start if I dare to say more.

A successful business to pass down which sounds like great news but it'd be no easy task to find someone to fill my shoes.

Tweedle Dee And Tweedle Dum

Tweedle Dee went to the café to buy some tea and Tweedle Dum preferred the liquor store for some rum.

But Tweedle Dee was wet with pee and Tweedle Dum had a cling on in his bum!

Then the café owner asked Tweedle Dee, ' why not use the bathroom, its free!'

But Tweedle Dee replied, ' it's too small and I need a pasture 'cause when nature calls, it's usually a disaster!'

Also the worker at the liquor counter asked Tweedle Dum, ' why not use the bathroom, pig?!'

And Tweedle Dum simply replied, ' it's too small to fit my behind and I didn't see the sign for a pig!

You dig?'

😑😲

A Short Visit

Once came a man or

twice?!?

I'm not sure?!?

Sashayed up to my deck as he probably did before, looking neither rich nor poor.

Peered through the window of my French style door, hoping to reel me in like a fish on a lure.

Only to find a lock fastened so secure, then he decided to drink his grandpa's medicine like a typical connoisseur!

So Be It!

If one refuses you,
so leave them!
Nobody is being you,
so just live it!
'Cause my true friends support me,
I love them!
If enemies talk behind my back,
so stab me!
When jealousy/ ignorance become them,
so sorry!
Inner peace and happiness,
I found them!
Life is beautiful,
so enjoy it!
And life goes on,
so be it!

Friend Unlimited

Fret thyself not!

Love you 'till I become a nought.

Like a sister you are.

So much we've been through so far!

Friends that hath no end, so here's something that I want to send.

A kiss or two, 'cause I'm thinking of you and a smiley face to brighten your day!

Tweedle Dee And Tweedle Dum

Tweedle Dee went to the café to buy some tea and Tweedle Dum preferred the liquor store for some rum.

But Tweedle Dee was wet with pee and Tweedle Dum had a cling on in his bum!

Then the café owner asked Tweedle Dee,

'why not use the bathroom? It's free!'

But Tweedle Dee replied, ' it's too small and I need a pasture 'cause when nature calls, it's usually a disaster!'

Also the worker at the liquor counter asked Tweedle Dum, ' why not use the bathroom? Pig! '

And Tweedle Dum simply replied, ' it's too small to fit my behind and I didn't see the sign for a pig! Ya dig?'

Church Revisited

A long time coming from a long time ago, At last, I mustered up the courage to go!

Came with a friend who frequents the mass like it's a trend.

Many seats vacant, why is it not so full?

Perhaps the younger crowd is tired of all the bull!

Not so much a fashion market, half dressed clothes of tattered and torn, kids with no shame, I don't get it.

God's holy house of unity and love but I still wonder if the priests truly accept me or somewhat sort of!

Revisiting the old church makes me feel blessed!

I see familiar faces and new faces and I must profess that it's such a wonderful feeling to reunite with a communal bunch that I'd love to join a few after the service for a meaningful lunch.

A Short Visit

Once came a man or
twice?!?
I'm not sure?!?
Sashayed up to my deck as he probably did before, looking neither rich nor poor.
Peered through the window of my French style door, hoping to reel me in like a fish on a lure.
Only to find a lock fastened so secure, then he decided to drink his grandpa's medicine like a typical connoisseur!

Okey Dokey!

I stoke the stove with the oak wood to heat my can of beans from Oakley while I'm taking note of the film about Annie Oakley.

I thought she came from a place called Muskogee, perhaps I made an error, it could be that I'm a little dopey!

I've done silly things like leaving my hands a little too soapy, dropping my oats all over the wood floor of oaky!

Now this makes me feel a bit mopey to have to clear the mess!

Oh well, oaky dokey!

Spare To Share

I can't live without my friends just like one can not live without air!

I think of them often and this is not a dare!

I say with total conviction that I love them all which is only fair!

'Cause time flies and we don't always have a moment to spare!

My love for my friends is beyond compare, It's such a bond that can't be measured anywhere!

Erfüllung